Carmen Mayer

Gymnastricks

Targeted Muscle Training For Dogs

Originally published in German by Kynos Verlag

English language edition first published 2017 by First Stone Publishing
An imprint of Westline Publishing Limited
The Old Hen House
St Martin's Farm
Zeals
Warminster
United Kingdom
BA12 6NZ

ISBN 9781 910488 42 3

© 2013 KYNOS VERLAG Dr. Dieter Fleig GmbH Konrad-Zuse-Straße 3, D-54552 Nerdlen/Daun

Printed by Printworks Global Ltd, London & Hong Kong.

The 'he' pronoun is used throughout this book instead of the rather impersonal 'it', however no gender bias is intended.

"Life is motion"

Aristotle

CONTENTS

Introduction

The tricks outlined in this book are all about building up specific muscle groups and keeping them in shape. They provide excellent preparation and warm-up routines before any kind of dog sport, improving balance, stability and body awareness.

In addition, they are highly beneficial for dogs that show muscular deficiencies due to illness or injury.

Before you start the gymnastricks programme, a detailed check-up by your dog's vet or physiotherapist should be considered absolutely essential.

However tempting it might be to get going right away, you need to talk to your vet or physiotherapist to find out which exercises will suit your dog and which ones you should avoid.

This is particularly important if your dog has specific health issues, if has undergone surgery, or if he is recovering from injury.

Each gymnastrick targets specific muscle groups. You can find an overview of the muscle groups (see page 13), along with the appropriate exercise/trick.

Never forget that each dog is an individual who will create his own version of the trick you are teaching. This will be dependent on his temperament and the way you are teaching the trick.

Therefore, it might be that other muscle groups are utilised as well as those that are targeted. This is not a problem as long as your dog is healthy, but it highlights the need to enlist the help of an expert before you get started.

In general, if your dog is finding an exercise difficult to perform or appears worried, stop training it.

Typically he will show his concern by using calming signals, such as turning his head to the side, yawning or tongue-flicking. In an extreme case, he will walk away to disengage himself from the training process.

Your dog may show a momentary reluctance, but his discomfort could be a sign of muscle hardening or some other physical problem.

Try training the exercise several days later. If your dog is still uneasy, consult your vet or physiotherapist again.

How To Teach Your Dog Gymnastricks

The gymnastricks programme is designed so that you can teach your dog progressively, step-by-step. There are two advantages to this method of training. Firstly, your dog's body can gradually adjust to the movement you are asking for; he is not being forced into position by following a treat.

Secondly, your dog actively engages in training; he has to think about what he is doing so he is using his brain as well as his body. In addition, if your dog hasn't completely understood the exercise, you can go back a step and establish the behaviour before progressing to the next stage.

The exercises are trained with the help of a clicker. Working with a target (a specific item that your dog should touch), and free shaping (your dog offering behaviours on his own initiative) play an important role in teaching gymnastricks.

However, if you are new to clicker training, you will still be able to follow the step-by-step instructions. If your dog is very experienced with clicker training, or is a very creative, you can skip some steps that are outlined for each exercise. But you may well find

that working through every stage helps your dog to get a concrete picture in his head, enabling him to fully understand what is required.

Of course, you can also train the exercises without the help of a clicker. For this, you can use a 'marker word' whenever a 'click' is mentioned in the instruction. A so-called 'marker word' performs the same function as a clicker, marking the moment when your dog is doing something correctly, and promising him a treat for his response.

To avoid confusion choose a word that you do not use in any other situation, such as "Yep", so your dog makes a clear connection. This system is not as precise as a clicker, but it does allow you to be hands-free.

Click for action, feed for position
Some clicker trainers use the saying: "click for action, feed for position" – and this is totally applicable for the gymnastricks programme. It means that you should always click your dog for an action he is performing and then feed him in that position.

So if you click your dog for the act of sitting down, i.e. for moving his bottom to the ground, you should then feed him in the sit. If you feed him when he is standing, after you clicked for the sit, you will most likely train your dog to sit for a short moment, and then to stand up to get his treat. In gymnastricks training, it is very important that your dog keeps his position. You know from your own fitness training that getting into a position is not the problem – it's staying there that counts!

So make sure you always "click for action, feed for position" when training the individual steps for each exercise. This is especially important as each end position of one step serves as the starting position for the next step. In some instances you have to react quickly to feed in the 'correct' position.

However, our dogs are very forgiving and most will get the idea even if our timing is not spot on. But try to see "click for action, feed for position" as your personal challenge while training the exercises; in this way, both you and your dog will be fine-tuning your skills.

Hand target
For many of the exercises in the gymastricks programme, your dog will need to know the hand target. A hand target is when your dog touches your hand with his nose. He learns to touch, on cue, regardless of where your hand is positioned. This gives you greater flexibility when training as you do not need to hold food in your hand to lure your dog; he will react to your hand as a target.

In order to teach the hand target, have your clicker and your treats ready:

• Offer your dog the flat palm of your hand, just in front of his nose. He will probably take an immediate interest, but you can attract him by tightening the muscles in your hand.
•   Click the first sign of interest and repeat several times. From the outset, offer your hand in a variety of positions – higher and lower, and to the side.
• Although your dog will probably regard your stretched-out palm as a cue, introduce a verbal cue, as this will help your dog to understand that he must touch your hand, regardless of where it is positioned.

All the exercises are taught in such a way that you can use everyday articles to train them. This includes, for example, books, stools, chairs, and blankets or small mats.

If you and your dog really get the fitness bug, you can buy fitness and rehab equipment for dogs, which includes balance cushions, exercise steps and wobble boards.

The dog's muscle groups

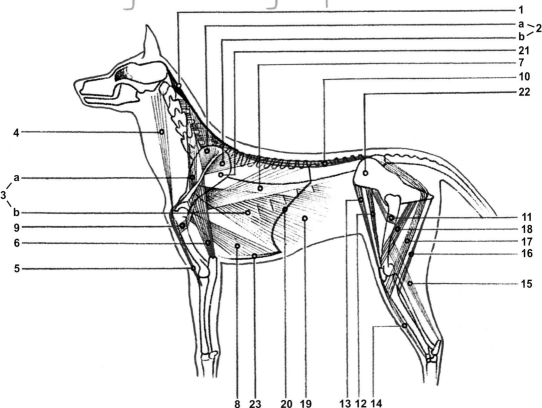

1. Nuchal ligament (Ligamentum nuchae)

2. Top shoulder muscle, trapezius muscle (musculus trapezius) [in green]

3. Undermost shoulder muscle (musculus serratus) [in blue]

4. Head-neck-arm muscle (musculus brachiocephalicus) [in green]

5. Flexors of the elbow joint (musculus biceps brachii) [in red]

6. Extensors of the elbow joint (musculus triceps brachii) [in red]

7. Wide back muscle, (musculus latissimus dorsi) [in green]

8. Breast muscle (musculus pectoralis) [in green]

9. Deltoid muscle (musculus deltoideus) [in orange]

10. Long back muscle (musculus longissimus) [in orange]

11. Flexors of the hip joint [in orange]

12. Extensors of the thigh [in blue]

13. Extensors of the knee joint [in red]

14. Flexors of the ankle joint [in green]

15. Extensors of the ankle joint musculus
    gastrocnemius) [in green]

16. Flexors of the knee joint (musculus biceps femoris) [in red]

17. - 18. Sprint muscles, musculus semitendinosus

19. Slant abdominal muscle [in green]

20. Diaphragm

21. Shoulder blade (scapula)

22. Hip bone (pelvis)

23. Breast bone (sternum)

9

Muscles and their function

1. Nuchal ligament (Ligamentum nuchae) [*black].
A long, slightly stretchable bowstring ligament that reaches from the axis to the first thoracic vertebra. It is attached to the third, fourth, fifth and sixth cervical vertebra and the first thoracic vertebra.
Function: It holds the neck and head in position and controls the movement of the head. It also serves as a connecting point of the muscles that produce the forward movement of the forelimb, as well as keeping the shoulder blades where they belong during the backward movement of the forelimb.

2. Top shoulder muscle, trapezius muscle (musculus trapezius) [*green].
This muscle consists of two parts. They are attached to the spine of the scapula, one at its front (a. into the direction of the head) and one at its back (b. in the direction of the body). The front part is connected to the nuchal ligament (beginning from the third or fourth cervical vertebra) and the first dorsal vertebrae. The back part is also attached between the second and ninth (or tenth) dorsal vertebrae.
Function: It keeps the tip of the shoulder blade in position, controls the movement of the upper part of the shoulder blade and is involved in the lifting and forward movement of the forelimb.

3. Undermost shoulder muscle (Musculus serratus) [*blue].
This muscle also consists of two parts: they are attached to the lower part of the spine of the scapula. One is attached to its front (a. in the direction of the head) and one at its back (b. in the direction of the body). The front part is also connected to the nuchal ligament (from the third cervical vertebra). The back part is attached to the ribs (extending to the seventh or eighth rib).
Function: The musculus serratus controls the movement of the lower part of the shoulder blade, takes part in moving the forelimb, carries the trunk and shoulder forwards and back, and depresses the scapula.
Activities of the musculus serratus and musculus trapezius are closely connected with each other: 2a and 3a, and 2b and 3b always work together.

4. Head-neck-arm muscle (Musculus brachiocephalicus) [*green].
This is a long muscle that reaches from the head of the humerus.
Function: This is the prime shoulder extensor. When the nuchal ligament is tensed and the head of the humerus is carried upwards, this muscle pulls up the forelimb by contracting itself. When the nuchal ligament is relaxed, contraction of the musculus brachiocephalicus pulls down the head of the humerus.

5. Flexors of the elbow joint (musculus biceps brachii) [*red].
A thin muscle that reaches from the lower part of the spine of the scapula in front of the head of the humerus and along the humerus towards the ulna.
Function: Flexes elbow, extends shoulder, provides passive stability when weight-bearing preventing shoulder flexion and keeps the head of the humerus where it belongs.

6. Extensors of the elbow joint (Musculus triceps brachii) [*red)].
A strong muscle that is attached to the spine of the scapula and the tip of the elbow.
Function: Extends the elbow joint and thereby the forelimb.

7. Wide back muscle (Musculus latissimus dorsi) [*green].
This is a broad muscle that is attached, at its back, to a big aponeurosis at the loins and at the last four dorsal vertebrae.
Function: Brings back the shoulder in collaboration with the breast muscle.

8. Breast muscle (Musculus pectoralis) [*green].
This muscle is attached to the breast-bone (sternum) and the under part of the ribs at one side, and to the head of the humerus at the other side.
Function: Brings back the shoulder in collaboration with the wide back muscle.

9. Deltoid muscle (Musculus deltoideus) [*orange].
Attached to the spine of the scapula and the upper part of the humerus.
Function: Flexes the deltoid.

10. Long back muscle (Musculus longissimus) [*orange].
This very important muscle is attached to all dorsal vertebrae from the loins to the neck.
Function: Forms the base of the nuchal ligament. Keeps the spine in place, allowing it to move, although other muscles also influence it. Allows the complete usage of thrust through the spine, carries a great amount of the body.

11. Flexors of the hip joint [*orange].
This muscle is attached to the hip-bones and the upper part of the femur.
Function: Flexes the hip joint.

12. Extensors of the thigh [*blue].
One end is attached to the hip bone and the other one to the lower part of the femur.
Function: Pulls the femur and thereby the hindlimb, forward.

13. Extensors of the knee joint [*red].
Reaches from the hip-bones to the head of the tibia.
Function: Keeps the knee straight during the forward movement of the hindlimb.

14. Flexors of the ankle joint [*green].
This muscle is attached to the tibia and the ankle joint.
Function: Flexes the ankle joint.

15. Extensors of the ankle joint (musculus gastrocnemius) [*green].
This muscle is attached to the under part of the tibia and is linked to the heel by the Achille's tendon.
Function: Extends the ankle joint.

16. Flexors of the knee joint (musculus biceps femoris) [*red].
This muscle is attached to the ischius and the tibia.
Function: It can flex the knee joint if the musculus semitendinosus is not working.

17. - 18. Sprint muscles (Musculus semitendinosus).
These are two strong muscles. Number 18 (*red) is attached to the hip joint and just above the knee joint. Number 17 (* blue) comes from the sacrum and reaches over the ischium to the head of the tibia. Both muscles reach around the knee joint, keeping it extended during the forward and backward movement of the leg.
Function: If the leg is extended forward on the floor, the muscles serve as shock absorbers. They then keep the knee joint extended, whereas the extensor of the ankle joint keeps the ankle joint extended. When the leg is placed on the ground, these muscles contract and thereby provide the thrust that is needed to move the body forward. Knee and ankle joint both have to be extended in order to achieve the greatest possible thrust.

19. Slant abdominal muscle [*green].
This muscle is attached to the ribs and to the aponeurosis of the lower belly.
Function: Controls the dog's breathing.

20. Diaphragm [*red]
The diaphragm is also called the thoracic diaphram and is a connective muscle tissue – a thin sheet of muscles that is located between the ribs. It is attached to the seventh rib and then stretches back to the end of the breast bone. At its top, it is attached to the loins.
Function: Controls the dog's breathing.

Exercises to target muscle groups

	Trunk muscles	Muscles of the knee joint	Hamstrings	Abductors	Muscles of the pelvis	Outer hip and croup muscles	Muscles of the elbow joint	Muscles of the carpal joint	Shoulder blade muscles	Deep shoulder girdle muscles	Breast muscle
Muscles of the back											
Standing on all 4 paws	X	X	X	X	X	X	X	X	X	X	
Standing with a stretched neck	X	X				X	X	X	X		
Down-Stand	X	X	X	X	X	X	X	X	X	X	X
Between your legs (with circular movement)	X	X	X	X	X	X	X	X	X	X	X
Standing on your feet	X	X	X	X	X	X	X	X	X		
Balancing on 2 legs (sideways)	X		X	X	X	X		X	X		X
Balancing on 2 legs (diagonally)	X		X	X	X	X		X	X		
Backwards slalom	X	X	X	X	X	X	X	X	X	X	X
Moving sideways	X	X	X	X	X	X	X	X	X	X	X
Slalom (with variations)	X	X	X	X	X	X	X	X	X	X	X
Abdominal muscles											
Sit-ups for dogs (dog lies on its side and moves its head to its flank)	X									X	X
Neck muscles											
Putting the head in your hand (hold)	X									X	
Looking downwards	X									X	
Down with the head	X									X	
Looking through the feet	X									X	X
Balancing a tray	X									X	X
Head towards flank	X									X	
Muscles of the forelimb (and muscles of the back)											
Digging	X						X	X	X	X	
Giving paws	X						X	X	X	X	
Lifting and holding a paw up	X						X	X	X	X	
Pushing paws against you	X						X	X	X	X	
Down-Sit and Sit-Down	X	X	X	X	X	X	X	X	X	X	
Collected sit	X		X		X	X					X
Stand – take a bow (and variations)	X						X	X	X	X	
Muscles of the hindlimb (and muscles of the back)											
Sit – Stand	X	X	X	X	X	X	X			X	X
Lifting a hind leg	X	X	X	X	X	X	X			X	X
Sit – Sitting up	X	X	X	X	X	X	X			X	X
Standing up with help	X	X	X	X	X	X	X	X	X	X	X
Standing up without help	X	X	X	X	X	X	X				
Walking backwards in a straight line	X	X	X	X	X	X	X		X	X	X
Ascending the stairs backwards	X	X	X	X	X	X	X	X	X	X	X
Down-take a bow	X	X	X	X	X	X	X	X			
All muscles											
Crawling	X	X	X	X	X	X	X	X	X	X	X
Balancing a tray on the back	X	X	X	X	X	X	X	X	X	X	X
Walking consciously	X	X	X	X	X	X	X	X	X	X	X
Change of pace: walk-trot, trot-walk	X	X	X	X	X	X	X	X	X	X	X
Looking forward while moving	X	X	X	X	X	X	X	X	X	X	X
Stepping under, Stretching legs	X	X	X	X	X	X	X	X	X	X	X

1. Core muscles

Back muscles

Standing on all four paws

An ideal exercise to start the gymnastricks programme is to teach your dog to stand with his weight deliberately placed on all four paws. This makes him aware of the static positioning of all his paws, but especially his hind paws.

Click your dog for climbing on the target with his hind paws.

Wait for all four paws to be placed on the target ...

... and only click then.

17

Targeted muscle groups:	Flexors and extensors of the front and hind legs, latissimus dorsi.
Suggested for:	Teaching concentration and relaxation.
Set-up of the exercise:	With this exercise, your dog will learn, first, to step up with his hind paws onto an elevated object and then to do the same thing with his front paws.
What is needed:	4 small targets. For beginner dogs, you should use a substantially elevated object, such as a number of books. For more experienced dogs, drip mats should work.

TRAINING STEP-BY-STEP

For beginners:

1. You will need two targets for this trick. Place both targets, ideally two books, next to each other. These are the targets for your dog's hind paws and should be large enough so that your dog can stand on them comfortably

2. Now it's time for your dog to get involved. He is likely to be interested in the objects on the floor so just let him follow you in a straight line over the targets. Click and reward when his hind legs touch the targets. To start with, click and reward when only one paw touches the target. Make sure you feed your dog in that position.

3. Guide your dog over the targets again, this time only clicking when both paws are standing on the targets.

Feed your dog in this position and repeat this part several times.

4. You are now ready to work on your dog's front paws. To do this you need to position two front paw targets directly in front of the hind-leg targets so that he can stand easily on both sets. Encourage your dog to walk over the targets, but only click him for touching the front paw targets – one paw is enough at this stage. Feed your dog when he is in the 'correct' position.

5. Next, click only for both front paws on the targets. Your dog should be standing with all his four feet on the four targets. You are now ready to move on to the exercise for advanced dogs.

Tip: If your dog is struggling to place his paws on the targets, make the exercise easier by giving him something bigger to aim for, such as an exercise step. This will help him with the concept that he has to "get on to something and stand there". Very often, the dog thinks that standing isn't enough and starts to offer other behaviours. Once he understands what is required, you can try again with the paw targets.

For more advanced dogs:

1. Position the hind leg targets so the gap between them equates to the gap between your dog's paws when he is standing normally. Now train the exercise as explained above, starting with the hind legs. Only click and reward when your dog makes a conscious decision to place his feet on the targets. This may take some time, but don't get impatient; this exercise calls for a lot of concentration and co-ordination.

2. If your dog manages to hit the hind paw targets, you can now move on to the front paw targets. Step by step, your dog is learning to position all four paws on the four individual targets.

3. Once your dog has understood this exercise, you can introduce a verbal cue, for example, "paws", just before the dog starts the exercise.

4. Now decrease the size of your targets; for example, you could use thinner books and then try sheets of paper. Once your dog can do the trick on a paper target, start to cut them into smaller and smaller pieces.

5. Gradually, try to fade out the targets until you don't need them at all. Your dog should now be able to respond to your verbal cue and place himself in the correct standing position.

Variations

To increase your dog's skills and promote balance and co-ordination, ask your dog to stand on a surface that is uneven or flexible. You can try working with a mattress, a trampoline or a deck chair.

Standing with stretched neck

When your dog stands with a stretched neck, it utilises the muscle groups of the front legs, shoulder and neck, as well as the back. In addition to stretching these muscles, it provides an ideal warm up exercise for dogs that compete in any activity that involves heelwork.

This is the correct position of your dog. You can see the bulge of the trapezius above the shoulder.

Getting ready: You can see the fore and hind-leg muscles being stretched, in addition to the back muscles while the dog is on tiptoe.

Targeted muscle groups:	Nuchal ligament, shoulder muscles, latissimus dorsi.
Suggested for:	Warm up before heelwork, stretching exercise for shoulder, neck and back muscles.
Set-up of the exercise:	Your dog will learn to stretch with the tip of his nose as high as possible while he stays in a standing position.
Prerequisite:	Hand target.

TRAINING STEP-BY-STEP

This gymnastrick is quick and easy to train, although the details are important!

1. Position your dog standing next to you, ideally in a heelwork position. Ask him to do a hand touch several times by offering your hand directly before his nose; click and reward. Make sure you hold your hand horizontal, level with your dog's nose.

2. If you dog is successful, offer your hand target a tiny bit higher every time you ask him to touch it. Imagine a quarter of a circle; the starting point is the tip of your dog's nose when he's looking straight ahead, the end point is when he's looking up with his nose in the air. Don't forget to click and reward each new point on the quarter circle at least three times, allowing your dog to adjust to the new

position. If your dog tries to sit down, you may have been asking too much, too soon. Go back a step and only click your dog while he's standing.

IMPORTANT NOTE:
If your dog repeatedly sits down, it could be that he is used to sitting down, or it could mean that he has tense muscles around his neck and shoulders. If you think it's just a habit, try turning your foot that is closest to your dog outward, so he would touch it if he tried to sit down. This should make him reconsider, so give lots of praise and extra treats for making the 'right' decision.

3. Now it's time to fine-tune the exercise. Observe your dog closely when you ask him to put his nose in the air (the end point of the quarter circle) and experiment with the height of your hand. For a full stretch, your dog should be on the tips of his toes, stretching the front part of his body towards your hand.

4. If he tries to jump up to get to your hand, just ignore him and go back to a lower position. For a full stretch, your dog will also need to use his hind legs and his back in order to stabilise his body so these muscle groups will also benefit.

Variations
To increase the benefit of this trick, first train it with your dog standing on four paws and then combine it with him stretching his neck. This variation can also help dogs that tend to sit down during training.

Tip: You can see how this exercise works on your body, too. While sitting, tilt your head so your nose is in the air, and you will feel the relevant muscles engaging. For maximum effect, try this with your hands and feet on the floor.

Down to stand

This gymnastrick can be compared to human press-ups; it targets not only the muscles of the upper arm and thigh, but also all the muscles of the back.

Ask your dog to lie down on a platform.

Be ready to click as soon as you see upwards movement from the hind legs.

23

Targeted muscle groups:	Latissimus dorsi, extensors and flexors of the hind legs, sprinter muscles.
Suggested for:	Strengthening your dog's muscles in general, especially good for weak hind legs.
Set-up of the exercise:	Changing from down to stand is an easy exercise to train, yet it is vital that your dog "folds" his legs in order to gain the utmost effect.
What is needed:	Platform.

TRAINING STEP-BY-STEP

1. It is easier to teach this exercise if you ask your dog to take up position on a platform. The starting position for this exercise is the down, where your dog has to lie down like a Sphinx. It is best to train this seated in front of your dog with your legs stretched out in the form of a V in order to contain your dog's sideways movement.

2. Start by offering a treat; for this trick, positioning is important so your dog does not go into a sit. Show the treat to your dog at floor level, directly in front of his nose, and then quickly move it upwards to your stomach. Follow a straight line, but move it in a sloping angle towards your stomach.

The end position of the treat is defined by the height of your dog's nose when standing. At first, only click your dog when he moves; watch his hind paws and click for any movement. Keep practising until he goes into a stand.

3. Now introduce a verbal cue, "stand". Gradually decrease the help you are giving, i.e. your legs are no longer in a V-position. Try to say the verbal cue first and only help with the treat if needed.

Variations
Your dog will get maximum benefit if he changes position from "stand" to "down" and "down" to "stand". Ideally, you would also train your dog to change into a "sit" and a "take a bow", he will then get be getting a whole-body work-out!

Between your legs (with circular movement)

This is an ideal way of training teamwork, and you can add lots of variations.

Use a hand target to guide the dog through your legs.

Here you can see that the dog has to bring herself into line in order to follow the circular movement of the handler.

Targeted muscle groups:	All core muscles.
Suggested for:	A warm-up for any kind of dog sport.
Set-up of the exercise:	Your dog learns to get into the position between your legs. He then learns to keep his position and to follow you in all directions.
Prerequisite:	Hand target.

TRAINING STEP-BY-STEP

1. Firstly, remind your dog of the hand target by asking him to touch your hand in several positions (for example, with your hand to your left, to your right, or when moving) and reward him for it.

2. Now turn around with your back to your dog. Leave some space between your legs, approximately as wide as your hips. Then offer a hand target by reaching your arm through your legs towards your dog. Don't look at your dog at this stage, as your body language might distract him from touching your hand.

3. When your dog touches your hand, click and reward by throwing a treat away from him, so that he has to walk through your legs to get it. While your dog is eating the treat, turn quickly in another direction so that you can repeat the exercise with the same starting position, Repeat until your dog is confidently walking through your legs.

4. When your dog is effortlessly touching your hand in this position, move your hand farther away, little by little. Click and reward each individual step by throwing the treat forward, which enables you to get back into the starting position.

5. Now place your hand on your belly button. Unless you have a giant breed, your dog will not be able to touch your hand in this position. Click and reward him for watching your hand. As this is the end result, feed your dog in this position rather than throwing the food.

6. Click and reward your dog several times for a steady stand in between your legs. Then give this gymnastrick a verbal cue, e.g. "get ready", and repeat a couple of times.

7. Take a short break and then go back to the starting position. Give your verbal cue and see if your dog responds. If he gets into position, click and reward him with lots of treats. If he does not know what to do, help him with the hand target and throw your treat forwards.

8. Once your dog is going into the correct position on cue, without needing the help of a hand target, you can start to move. Try a step at a time and if your dog moves with you, click and reward him instantly. Only ask for easy forward movement to begin with. Start walking in big circles, and then gradually decrease them in size. Now try walking in the other direction.

The big advantage of this gymnastrick is that you can actively guide your dog's movement and thereby influence the bend of his spine, depending on his flexibility.

Variations
This exercise also works with sideways or backwards movements, although your dog should know these directional movements before you try.

Standing on your feet

With this exercise, you are teaching your dog to move with back-end awareness. He thereby achieves a high level of co-ordination and balance. It is of special benefit to dogs that do not have good back end awareness, and for strengthening hind leg muscles. This exercise requires a lot of trust: if your dog does not feel completely comfortable, he could tend to tighten up, which would be counter-productive.

Turn your feet inwards to make it easier for your dog to stand on them.

With practice, your dog will be able to maintain his balance when you are moving.

Targeted muscle groups:	Latissimus dorsi, extensors and flexors of the hind leg.
Suggested for:	Mobilising the hind legs.
Set-up of the exercise:	Your dog learns to stand on your feet and to follow your movements.
What is needed:	Post-its.
Prerequisite:	Standing between your legs.

TRAINING STEP-BY-STEP

The set-up is very similar to the previous exercise where your dog stands between your legs.

1. Stand and face your dog. Ask your dog to come between your legs, but turn your feet inwards.

2. With this positioning your dog will, unintentionally, touch your feet. This is the moment you want to click and reward. A mere touch is enough to start with; your dog doesn't have to stand on your feet straightaway. Click this first touch several times, making sure your dog is in the correct

position. After about five clicks, throw the treat forwards so that your dog leaves the position he is in.

3. Now turn 180 degrees so that your dog approaches you from behind. Turn your feet inwards so that your dog has to step on to them. Click the first paw touch and give him a big treat.

4. Now wait to see if he puts his other paw on to your other foot as well. If he hesitates, help him by offering a hand target which will encourage him to put his other paw on your foot. Take care not to squeeze your dog between your legs. If you sense that he is feeling uncomfortable, go back and re-train this position.

5. When your dog is returning to the correct position after you have thrown a treat, it's time to introduce a verbal cue, e.g. "feet".

6. You can now slowly straighten your feet and ask your dog to get on them with the help of your verbal cue. If this poses a problem, just go back one training step and then try again.

7. When your dog is eager to get into position, you can try to move your feet. Start with one foot at a time and only move it slightly forward. If your dog stays in position, click and treat him.

8. Now move your other foot and continue as described above. This is nitty-gritty work: vary the length of your stride and reward your dog for keeping his position. You can then 'feel' how your movement affects your dog's hind leg movement and adjust accordingly.

Variations

For dogs that have problems putting their paws on to their handler's feet, try using small post-it notes. Place a post-it on the floor and teach your dog to touch it with his paw. If this works, move the post-it from the floor to your foot. Do this when your dog is in position between your legs – he will soon learn that he has to put his paw on your foot. Have fun!

Balancing on two legs (sideways)

Balancing on two legs is very challenging, but even more co-ordination and strength is needed in order to to balance on two legs diagonally.

Initially use a shallow item (e.g. a book) as a hind paw target.

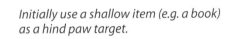

The target needs to be higher (e.g. two books).

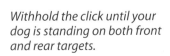

Withhold the click until your dog is standing on both front and rear targets.

Targeted muscle groups:	Shoulder muscles, wide dorsal muscle (pectoralis major), breast muscle, outer hip and croup muscles (on one side of the body).
Suggested for:	Strengthening your dog's torso, enhancing co-ordination and balance.
Set-up of the exercise:	With the help of two elevated platforms, your dog will first learn to use his paws individually. You will then teach him that the mere lifting of the paws will earn him treats, and from there, you can start to shape the balancing exercise.
What is needed:	Front and hind paw targets, e.g. books.
Prerequisite:	Walking backwards, see page 99.

TRAINING STEP-BY-STEP

For this exercise, your dog needs to walk backwards and he needs to understand the concept of stepping on to a target mat. For detailed instructions, see walking backwards in a straight line, page 99.

1. Start with your dog standing in front of you and place a small item, such as a book, behind one of his hind legs. (It does not matter what item you use as long as it's higher than ground level.) Now ask your dog to walk backwards. Make sure you click the moment your dog steps on to the elevated item, and reward him. If your dog does not hit the target, reposition it and try again. Repeat several times.

2. Once the dog understands that he must walk backwards and step on to the elevated item, gradually increase the height of the target, for example by adding a second small book. Continue to click and reward your dog for putting his paw on to the elevated item.

3. Depending on the size of your dog, you will need to increase the height of the target several times so that he learns to lift his leg to the correct height.

4. You can now click just before your dog puts his paw down on to the elevated target. Work on shaping this movement with precision – that is, while his paw is still in the air.

5. If your dog is successful, introduce a verbal cue for lifting his leg, such as "back lift". When you have done this, you are almost there.

6. Repeat the steps described above, but this time you are teaching your dog to lift his front paw (on the same side as the back paw "lift"). Position the target directly behind your dog's front leg and train him to lift his leg by clicking and rewarding until you can ask him on a verbal cue, such as "front lift".

Depending on your dog, you can now proceed in one of two ways:

1. Fade out the targets that serve as a trigger for the new behaviour, and then give your verbal cues.

2. Give your verbal cues for both legs and then fade out the targets afterwards. If your verbal cues are strong enough, getting rid of the targets should not pose a problem.

Do not expect too much of your dog. Not only is this exercise very intense in terms of coordination and concentration, it is also physically exhausting as your dog is learning a new way of moving and balancing.

Tip: You can help your dog by standing next to him so he can lean towards you in order to get into position – just try and see what your dog likes best!

Balancing on two legs (diagonally)

Balancing on two legs is very challenging, but even more co-ordination and strength is needed in order to to balance on two legs diagonally.

Put the second target diagonally in relation to the first one.

Reward your dog for putting his feet on the diagonal targets.

34

From now on, your dog must lift his legs to earn a click.

Targeted muscle groups:	Shoulder muscles, wide dorsal muscle (pectoralis major), breast muscle, outer hip and croup muscles (on the diagonal side).
Suggested for:	Strengthening your dog's torso, enhancing coordination and balance.
Set-up of the exercise:	As in teaching your dog to balance on two legs sideways, you train him to step on two elevated items. Then you click him for lifting his paws before putting them down on the items. After that you combine the lifting of two paws diagonally.
What is needed:	Items for your dog to step on to, such as books.
Prerequisite:	Walking backwards, page 99.

TRAINING STEP-BY-STEP

Train as for the previous exercise, but now you are working on your dog's right front and left hind leg, or vice versa.

Introduce a specific verbal cue for each leg, such as "front-right/"back left". This allows you to ask for them individually, or in combination, which enlarges your repertoire for later exercises.

Variations

For the ultimate mental and physical workout, ask your dog to alternate his two balancing exercise, i.e. balance sideways and then balance diagonally. Make sure both behaviours are well established before attempting this otherwise he will get confused.

Backwards slalom

This gymnastrick stimulates flexion of the spinal cord; in addition your dog has to engage his back end, manoeuvring it between your legs. This exercise is very tiring, especially for dogs that are not used to learning tricks. You therefore need to progress slowly, over a period of time, allowing your dog to build up strength and flexibility, and to improve his co-ordination.

Adopt the start position (see page 40) and place some treats on the feeding station.

Your dog will pause after eating the treats…

…and leave his position backwards. At this moment, you should click.

Feed your dog next to your leg.

38

Practise this on either side.

The dog is now turning around the leg, rear-end first.

Targeted muscle groups:	Latissimus dorsi
Suggested for:	Dogs that have no back end awareness; requires a great deal of lateral flexion of the spinal cord.
Set-up of the exercise:	With the help of a feeding station, your dog will learn to walk backwards through your legs. The angle of the gate you are forming with your legs will then change step by step in order for your dog to bend.
What is needed:	An object that is the same height as your dog's head, for example a stool or a chair that can act as a feeding station.

TRAINING STEP-BY-STEP

1. Start with your dog in a sit, approximately two metres from the feeding station.

2. Position yourself in front of the feeding station with your toes touching it. To allow room for your dog, your feet should be hip-width apart. Put a treat on the chair and have a clicker and treats ready

3. Call your dog through your legs to the feeding station, where he can eat the treat you have put out.

4. Now it gets interesting... Once your dog has eaten the treat he will want to leave so he will, in all probability, take a step backwards. This is the crucial moment: click your dog for the backwards movement and reward from behind you.

Tip: If your dog tries to leave the feeding station by moving forward, place some cushions around the chair/stool so that he cannot escape to the front or side.

5. For a few repetitions, you need to turn yourself into a into a 'treat machine'. At this stage you still need the treat on the feeding station to position your dog; the treat you offer for backwards movement (given behind you) is rewarding the new behaviour. It is

a good idea to offer different value treats to mark this. The treat on the feeding station could be low value kibble, whereas the treat behind your back could be high value cheese or liver. Repeat this step several times, in order to generate fluid movement.

6. Once this movement sequence is established, you need to stand further back from the feeding station. This should be done gradually so one step back will be fine to begin with. Start with your dog in a sit and place the treat before you go to your start position.

7. Continue this moving-away procedure, with the dog offering backwards movement, until he is standing between your legs.

8. You can now start the process of turning. Remember to move one leg only; the other remains static. The end position is for your legs to form a gate, but you need to progress to this stage. It doesn't matter which leg you begin with, as long as you always use the same leg when training. In this instance, let's start with the right leg and imagine that you are going to trace a quarter of a circle behind the other leg. Position your right leg a small step backward on the quarter circle; at this stage keep the movement minimal so you are not asking for too much. Position yourself so that when your dog walks

backwards, he will touch your right leg. This is the moment you want to click. Reward your dog for touching your leg and correcting his trajectory. Repeat this step several times.

9. Now take another step, moving your leg back a little bit more. If this works, you can take your leg back a step further until it is on the same line as your other leg. Make sure you reward for every stage.

10. Once your dog can move backwards away from the feeding station and turn his rear end so that he finishes between your legs, you can introduce a verbal cue. It is helpful to combine two signals. You could, for example, use "zag" for the left side and "zig" for the right side.

11. You can now reward your dog next to the leg you didn't move (in this instance, the left leg.

You have now trained one side and taught your dog a verbal cue for this side. No worries, the other side will be trained much quicker!

12. Go back to the beginning. You can now move your other leg (in our example, the left leg) and introduce a verbal cue for that side.

13. Next, you can put the backward slalom together. You need to have your dog right next to you, either in the left or right heel position. Forget about where you placed your legs in the previous steps and follow this guideline: the leg that is farthest away from the dog moves backwards first. Cue your dog for the side you want, but remember that your verbal cue means "bend to the left" or "bend to the right" for your dog, irrespective of the leg you used beforehand. If you have moved your right leg back first and have cued your dog's movement with the word "zag", your dog has learned to bend left (use "zig" for the right side because of the "i" – it's easier to remember). If this works, reward your dog generously.

14. Now try the other side. If your dog is successful, you can start to put both sides together to form a backward slalom – a brilliant exercise to teach your dog back end awareness.

Variations
This exercise is especially useful in that you can ask for each side individually, meaning you can actively train one side or spice up your heelwork by using backward slalom angles in order to change position.

Moving Sideways

This gymnastrick is designed to promote the co-ordination and flexibility of the entire back. If your dog has problems with this exercise, it could well be that he is a little stiff so you will need to take things slowly.

Here you can see the start position.

The dog brings himself into line, in front of his handler. With the help of the cushion, the effect on his back muscles clearly increases.

Targeted muscle groups:	Latissimus dorsi, pectoris major.
Suggested for:	To promote co-ordination and flexibility in general, and, especially of the lumbar portion of the spine.
Set-up of the exercise:	First of all, you have to mobilise your dog's rear end. Once he understands this, you can create a logical sequence leading to moving sideways.
What is needed:	A small box or a balance cushion that serves to elevate your dog's front paws.
Prerequisite:	Hand target.

This is hard work, not only for the hind legs.

Now try the exercise without the cushion.

Note the sequence of sideways movement.

TRAINING STEP-BY-STEP

1. For this exercise you need a small box or a balance cushion. Initially click and reward your dog for showing interest in the item – no matter how small. In time, your dog will start to use his paws in order to interact with it. This is the moment for a jackpot reward!

2. Make sure your dog keeps both front feet on the cushion while you feed him. If your dog is reluctant to stay in position, help him with a hand target. Stand directly in front of your dog. When he has both paws on the cushion, offer a hand target, positioning it so he can reach it comfortably in the stand. Repeat this at least five times.

3. You can then start to move in a circle around the cushion. Start with tiny steps so that your dog only has to move his head. Click and reward him.

4. Now move slightly further away from your dog, but still in the same direction. Keep offering the hand target, which will help your dog to focus and to start turning. It is important to click his rear end movement. As soon as he moves his rear sideways, click and reward. Repeat this several times.

5. Now use the same procedure to train the other direction. Once your dog is following you in both directions, create duration by rewarding him after every two or three steps. Vary directions and the rate of treats.

6. If your dog is following you for several steps in both directions, it's time to introduce a verbal cue for moving sideways in a circle. It is best to choose two signals, one for walking sideways to the left, e.g. "go left", and one for walking sideways to the right, ("go right"). Cue your dog, and then start to move. Click and reward for a correct response. In this way, your dog will start to link the cue with the behaviour and will begin to move immediately after the verbal cue.

7. Now progress to asking for the gymnastrick without the aid of a

Tip: If your dog doesn't move his rear end, help him by moving your target hand towards his shoulder. He should follow this movement and thus, involuntarily, move his hind legs. Click and treat this several times.

balance cushion or small box. Ask for the exercise on the elevated item first and then remove it. Position yourself in front of your dog and give your verbal cues, just as if the item was still there. Reward your dog for every tiny step he is making, because you have increased the difficulty by removing the visual aid.

8. First, decide which direction you want to focus on. Then give your verbal cue but instead of moving in a circle, move a little bit to the side. If your dog needs some help, use a hand target, but he should know by now what you want him to do. Click and treat when he moves his rear end and show him how happy you are that he has understood the concept!

9. Now move in bigger steps and change direction. Well done!

Variations

You have taught your dog how to walk sideways in front of you. In order to make this exercise more interesting, you can change your position in relation to your dog, although this only works with a well-established verbal cue. You can also add some distance between you and your dog with the help of a barrier. In addition, you can combine walking sideways with asking him to stop in a stand position, and then giving the command for the other side.

Tip: If your dog is struggling with the abrupt removal of the elevated item, go back to using it, then train with progressively smaller items. A mouse mat is ideal as the last step before you ask your dog to do the exercise on the ground.

If your dog follows you in every direction and with every step you take, you can start to train the sideways movement – but now your dog knows how to use his rear end.

Slalom
(with variations)

The slalom is a great trick as you can fine-tune the degree to which your dog bends his spine and how quickly he does it. The slalom between the legs, and its variations , are ideal exercises to warm up your dog before any kind of sporting activity.

1.

Guide your dog through the legs with a hand target.

2.

Your dog will soon work without the help of a hand target.

3.

Here you can see how the dog has to bend his spine for this exercise.

Targeted muscle groups:	Latissmus dorsi, pectoris major.
Suggested for:	An ideal warm-up exercise where you can control the intensity. Especially good for training the flexibility of the spine.
Set-up of the exercise:	Your dog learns to weave through your legs. The position you're feeding your dog in is very important here, as it's the starting position for the next weave.

TRAINING STEP-BY-STEP

1. Stand next to your dog and step forward on the leg that is farthest from your dog, i.e. if your dog is standing to the left of you, choose the right leg, and vice versa.

2. Now offer your dog your hand target according to the leg you have moved forward: right leg means right hand. Position your hand between your legs, palm facing outwards. Click and reward your dog for touching your hand. It is important to throw treats away from you but in the correct direction, making sure that your dog walks through the 'gate' you are forming with your legs. If your dog has trouble seeing the hand target, move it a little to help him. You may need to repeat this step several times.

3. When your dog clearly understands what you want, move him closer to your thigh. Feed him directly from the hand target so that he stands parallel to your leg.

4. When this behaviour is established, introduce a verbal cue for this side. For example, you could use "sla-" for left to right and "lom" for right to left.

5. Test your dog by letting your hand target rest on your thigh and just giving him the verbal cue. If this works, train the other side following the preceding steps. Make sure you feed your dog parallel to your leg, which will enable you to put both sides together more easily.

Once your dog has learned both sides, ask for both of them, one after the other, and vary the reward rate.

Variations
The individual sides of the slalom, and the slalom itself, offer lots of training variations:

- Ask for each slalom step individually so your dog changes from the left to the right heelwork position or vice versa.

- Ask your dog to "wait" after going under each leg in order to control his speed.

- Vary the length of your stride to influence how much your dog has to bend.

- Work different speeds, walking or trotting, helping your dog with slower or faster verbal cues.

- Try a slalom where you both move to the side. For your dog, the exercise remains the same, except that you cross your legs and thereby vary the movement between tight and loose bending.

Abdominal muscles

Sit-Ups

In this gymnastrick, the dog lies on his side and lifts his head to his flank. Just as with human sit-ups, the dog's abdominal muscles get a work-out!

Here you can see how the post-it facilitates the exercise.

Note the stretching required in the upper part of the body.

Targeted muscle groups:	Latissimus dorsi, pectoralis major, breast muscle, abdominal muscle.
Suggested for:	Stretching the entire forequarters. Helps to tone the stomach.
Set-up of the exercise:	In this exercise, the dog learns to touch his flank with his head while he is lying down.
What is needed:	Post-it or a small hairgrip.

TRAINING STEP-BY-STEP

1. Make yourself comfortable on the floor with your dog. For this exercise, the dog should lie on his side. Depending on the nature of your dog's coat, you should choose a post-it or a hairgrip to stick or clip into his fur. It shouldn't be uncomfortable for your dog, just something to arouse his interest.

2. Have your clicker and some treats ready, and position the post-it or hairgrip on your dog's thigh. Click and reward for any interest he shows and feed him as he reaches for his thigh.

3. Repeat this a few times and over a number of training sessions. Also train the other side.

4. Once you are starting to get what you want, introduce a verbal cue for each side.

5. Wait until your dog understands the cue and then slowly fade the triggering object.

Variations
The longer the dog can stay in position, the stronger the effect. So slowly try to withhold the click in order to lengthen the duration of the trick.

Neck Muscles

Hold

The dog drops his head into your hand and maintains the position for an extended period of time. In this way, he is able to relax his neck muscles or, depending on the position, stretch them. This is a useful calming exercise for high-energy dogs. It is also beneficial for dogs that use their neck muscles a lot, for example when working in the heel position.

Initially, the dog is simply resting his head, but gradually he transfers the full weight of it.

51

Note how the dog is increasingly allowing the weight of his head to be supported.

Targeted muscle groups:	Nuchal ligament, shoulder muscle, head-throat-arm muscle.
Suggested for:	Relaxing, and for dogs that often work in the heel position.
Set-up of the exercise:	In this exercise, you lure the dog with a treat. He learns that only by dropping his head into your hand will he get the treat.

TRAINING STEP-BY-STEP

1. For this exercise, you need to work at your dog's level. He can work from any position but he will be more comfortable, and you can therefore increase duration, if he is lying down.

2. Show your dog that you have some really tasty treats for him today, but don't give him one.

3. Close up your hand so that your palm forms a hollow. This will be the resting place for your dog's head. Have a treat ready in your other hand.

4. Show your dog the treat and position the hollow of your palm so he only has to move his head a little to drop into it as he focuses on the treat. You may have to play with the positioning of the treat to get the correct response. The moment your dog touches the hollow of your palm, click and reward. From the very beginning, make sure his entire muzzle is lying in your hand to give him the right idea. Repeat this step a couple of times.

5. Now your dog needs to lay his head more heavily in your hand. You can achieve this by withholding the click and reward for a few seconds. You can also try to hold the treat a bit lower down. At this stage you need to move on in very small steps. The dog shouldn't remove his muzzle from the hollow of your hand; he just should look downward and thereby put more pressure into your hand. Click at this exact moment and allow your dog to eat the treat in this position. Repeat this step until your dog has a clear understanding of what you want him to do.

6. Now try to hold the palm of your hand lower down. You might have to wait until he is in position and then move your hand a bit lower. See if he follows you.

7. Start giving the exercise a verbal cue, e.g. " hold", and use fewer treats to increase duration.

Variations

Train this trick in a standing and sitting position, and try to extend the length of time that the dog stays in position by clicking later. The longer he can maintain this position, the more beneficial it will be for his neck muscles. When he closes his eyes, you know you and he are pros!

Looking down

Looking down is an ideal way for your dog to stretch his neck muscles and the muscles of his back. It's a good exercise to provide balance for a dog that does a lot of heelwork.

If the dog stands on a platform, it increases the stretching effect of the exercise.

Targeted muscle groups:	Nuchal ligament, shoulder muscle, head-throat-arm muscle, long back muscle.
Suggested for:	A balance exercise for dogs which often use their neck muscles.
Set-up of the exercise:	The dog learns to touch a target on the floor with his nose while standing. When you are feeding the dog in this position and taking the target away slowly, he will often look down to the floor.
What is needed:	Target (e.g. a post-it), a platform for the dog to stand on.

TRAINING STEP-BY-STEP

1. For this gymnastrick, the dog should be in a standing position which prevents him from lying down to touch the target. It may help to position the dog on a step. Get ready with your clicker, treats and a post-it (for the target).

2. Show your dog the target and click and reward him as soon as he touches it with his nose. If your dog likes to use his paw, hold the target high enough that he cannot touch it.

3. If this works well, move the target slowly towards the floor. Don't forget to click and reward all the small steps in-between.

4. Now stick the post-it on the floor, just in front of your dog's paw. It should not be too far away from him, nor too close, as he needs to be able to reach it from the stand.

5. Click and reward for nose touches only. The place where you reward your dog is very important here. Don't feed your dog on the target, feed him high up, so that he has to lift his head. This will also prevent him from lying down.

6. When your dog has eaten the treat, he will look back down to the target. Click that and reward, again feeding him high up.

7. Just before your dog looks down, introduce a verbal cue, e.g. "look down".

8. It's time to make the post-it a bit smaller – but don't do this too fast. To keep your dog interested in the smaller target, occasionally feed him on the target.

9. Now try to get rid of the post-it completely. Click your dog at the lowest point of his movement. He will automatically look up again and there he will find his reward.

Variations

Vary your dog's position – he will get maximum benefit if he is sitting. Additionally you can increase duration, by waiting a bit longer until you click. It helps if your dog has already learned from other tricks to stay in one position, similar to the 'Hold' exercise (see page 51).

Head down

In the exercise, your dog learns to drop his head down to the floor while he is lying down. When your dog is in the sphinx position and presses his head right down to the floor, it gives his neck and back muscles a really good stretch.

The hand signal, which indicates "hold", can be faded when the dog is in position.

The inflated pillow increases the effect of the exercise because the dog has to balance his entire weight while his head is positioned on the floor.

Targeted muscle groups:	Nuchal ligament, shoulder muscle, head-throat-arm muscle, long back muscle.
Suggested for:	Stretching the neck and as relaxation for high-energy dogs.
Set-up of the exercise:	If he knows the cue "hold", your dog understands the concept of lying his head down, so it's very easy to train the "down".
Prerequisite:	Hold, see page 51.

TRAINING STEP-BY-STEP

1. Ask your dog to lie on the floor in the sphinx-position. Give the verbal cue "hold" (see page 51), holding the palm of your hand (forming a hollow) between his front legs. Click and reward when he puts his head in your hand. Repeat several times.

2. Now put your hand on the floor and ask for "hold" again. As your dog lowers his head, take away your hand so that he touches part of it, but mostly touches the floor. Click and give a big reward if he gets it right. If he is a bit confused, just go back one step.

3. Now remove your hand entirely. If your dog touches the ground, click and reward him.

4. When you are confident that your dog fully understands this gymnastrick, without the aid of your hand, you can add a verbal cue, e.g. " head down".

Variations
For maximum benefit, you can elevate your dog's rear end by using a cushion or a balance cushion.

Looking through the feet

This is a really complex trick which involves all-round stretching engaging the back, neck and shoulder muscles. It's just like when you round your back and look through your legs. In addition to the relaxing effect, it's a good contrapuntal movement for dogs who work in the heel position.

Click the first moment your dog shows interest in the post-it.

Here you can see how much the back has to bend.

Your dog will soon be doing this exercise on his own!

Targeted muscle groups:	Nuchal ligament, shoulder muscle, head-throat-arm muscle, long back muscle.
Suggested for:	Dogs that often work in the heel position, and for stretching the back and neck muscles.
Set-up of the exercise:	Similar to the trick "looking at the floor". The dog learns to look under his belly through his legs with the help of a target.
What is needed:	An elevated platform the size of your dog, post-its.
Prerequisite:	Looking down, see page 54.

TRAINING STEP-BY-STEP

1. To help your dog to remain in the standing position for this exercise, ask him to stand on an elevated surface, such as a step.

2. Start with the 'looking down' trick (see page 54) so your dog gets the idea.

3. Take a post-it and hold it directly underneath your dog. Do this by putting your hand through his back legs in order to trigger the right movement. When your dog shows interest in what you are doing under his belly, click and reward him. It is very important to feed him in this position.

4. Now stick the post-it just a little bit in front of your dog's back paw. If he shows no interest, point your finger towards the post-it or help him with a treat. Click his first look towards the target. At this stage, you are not expecting him to touch the target

(which he couldn't do anyway). Sitting down or moving away is almost impossible, because he is on a platform.

5. Keep working to get a really round back; the exercise should not be confined to simply looking through the front legs alone.

6. When your dog fully understands what is required, add a verbal cue and gradually fade out the post-it.

Variations
You can give your dog an even better stretch if his front feet are higher than his back feet. You can do this with the aid of a small platform.

Balancing a bowl

In this fun gymnastrick, your dog learns to balance an object on his head. This exercises his neck and shoulder muscles, and helps to prevent stiffness. Choose an object that has a large flat surface which fits the size of your dog's head.

Place a small item on your dog's head.

Slowly withdraw the supporting hand.

61

Increase the distance between you and your dog.

Ask your dog to walk towards you.

62

Targeted muscle groups:	Nuchal ligament, shoulder muscle, head-throat-arm muscle.
Suggested for:	A fun exercise that works the neck muscles.
Set-up of the exercise:	This exercise takes a long time to learn but it's very good for teaching body awareness. To start with, ask your dog to "hold" (see page 51), and then follow the step-by-step instructions to get him to balance the bowl on his head.
What is needed:	A lightweight bowl, or a similar item that has a flat base, plus a chair.
Prerequisite:	The 'hold' trick.

TRAINING STEP-BY-STEP

1. The best way to start this exercise is to sit on a chair with your dog sitting in front of you. Ask your dog for the 'hold' (see page 51). Click and reward him.

2. While your dog has his head in your hand, place the object (in this instance a bowl) on his head and hold it in place. Click and reward him for staying still.

3. Once your dog is comfortable with the bowl on his head, you no longer need to hold it in position. Click and reward your dog for waiting calmly.

4. Now you can gradually try to reduce the amount of help you give with your "hold" hand, i.e. where your dog is resting his head. Remove one finger at a time, rewarding at every stage, until your dog is sitting quietly with the bowl on his head, with no assistance from you. For this trick, you do not need a verbal cue as your dog should know what to do when you appear with the bowl.

Variations
Try doing the exercise while your dog is standing. If that goes well, encourage him to move forward a few steps. Once he can do that, he has earned a big jackpot!

Head to the side

This is a very beneficial exercise which stretches the thoracic vertebra starting from the neck muscles. Stiffness in the neck and shoulder girdle often extend to the thoracic vertebra muscles, and this is a good exercise for loosening them. It is useful for dogs that work in the heel position, but this exercise is a good warm-up for all kinds of sports in which the spine bends sideways, such as around jumps in agility, the turn in flyball, or a fast leg weave in freestyle.

Be ready to click your dog when he shows interest in the target.

Progress to clicking when he moves his head, and gradually fade out the target.

Targeted muscle groups:	Nuchal ligament, shoulder muscles, head-throat-arm-muscles, breast muscles, broad back muscle.
Suggested for:	Stretching the neck and thoracic vertebra muscles. Ideal warm-up exercise for all dog sports.
Set-up of the exercise:	Like the dog sit-ups, this teaches your dog to move his head to the side. To make it easier, position the dog between your legs.
What is needed:	Post-it or a small hairgrip.
Prerequisite:	A stand (between your legs).

TRAINING STEP-BY-STEP

1. Position your dog between your legs so that his hip is level with your legs. Bend your knees slightly, so that you are nearly sitting on his backside.

2. Depending on the length of your dog's coat, choose a post-it or hairgrip to stick or clip on to his thigh. This should not be uncomfortable for your dog; it just should arouse his interest.

3. Get your clicker and some treats and position the post-it or hairgrip on his thigh. Make sure that your dog is standing straight. You can use your legs to help him stay in position, but you should never push or squeeze him. He should always feel comfortable.

4. Click and reward your dog for showing any interest in the post-it and feed him when his head is turned towards it. Repeat this a few times over a number of training sessions. Also train the other side.

5. Once your dog understands the routine, you can introduce a verbal cue for each side. Wait until your dog has made the connection with the cue and then slowly fade out the triggering object, i.e. the post-it/hairgrip.

Variations
Benefit is accrued by maintaining this position, so build up duration by delaying the click and the reward.

2. Forelimb muscles

(plus back muscles)

Digging

Digging is an ideal exercise for strengthening your dog's foreleg muscles and giving his forequarters a workout.

Targeted muscle groups:	Shoulder muscles, foreleg extensors and flexors, chest muscles, *latissimus dorsi*.
Suggested for:	Working the forequarters as a good warm-up for the muscles located there, in order to prevent injuries. This is particularly useful for sports in which the front legs take a pounding, such as agility and flyball. In addition, it builds shoulder muscles.
Set-up of the exercise:	Get your dog to dig by using a blanket as the basis for the training.
What is needed:	Blanket.

TRAINING STEP-BY-STEP

For this gymnastrick you will need a clicker, some treats and a blanket.

1. Put the blanket in a heap on the floor in front of you to encourage your dog to focus on it. Use the clicker when he shows interest and reward him with a treat placed on the blanket.

2. Wait to see if he paws the blanket. If he does, click and treat. If he doesn't, help him by pointing at the blanket or by 'pawing' it with your hands. You can try hiding treats under the blanket, although some dogs tend to use their nose instead of their paws to find them.

3. When your dog understands that he needs to paw the blanket, withhold the click and the treats. This will make him try harder so he will start to dig the blanket, which is exactly what we want. Click and give a big reward.

4. When your dog has understood the exercise, introduce a verbal cue, e.g. "dig'". Since most dogs enjoy digging, this should not take too long.

5. You can now transfer the exercise to a smaller blanket, to a rug, or take it outside and ask your dog to "dig" the ground. Your dog needs to learn that he should dig when he is given the verbal cue, regardless of where he is and without focusing on a specific object.

Variations
Your dog will dig harder if he has to use more force. You can facilitate this by providing a sandbox or something similar for him to dig in.

Giving paws

Teaching a dog to give alternate paws is
quite simple but very useful for working
on foreleg muscles through to the back.

Begin by offering your fist…

…then hold out your hand.

In order to balance, the dog has moved his right hind leg forward.

Targeted muscle groups:	Shoulder muscles, extensor and flexor foreleg, chest muscles, latissimus dorsi.
Suggested for:	Using the front muscles of the forepaws. As an ideal start to a warm-up programme. When the dog is asked to give paws at random, it is mentally stimulating.
Set-up of the exercise:	By hiding a treat in your hand, you can get your dog to use his paws, and then add a command.

TRAINING STEP-BY-STEP

1. Sit in front of your dog. Hide a treat in your fist, palm down, and offer it to your dog near his paws.

2. Click when he touches your hand with his paw – do not click when he touches with his nose. Reinforce this paw action by clicking and treating several times.

3. Now turn your fist over so that the back of your hand points down, and treat your dog when he touches your hand.

4. Remove the treat from your hand and click and treat when your dog touches your empty fist. Use your other hand to reward the dog.

5. Just before your dog uses his paw again, open your fist so that he touches the palm of your hand. Click and treat this several times and introduce a verbal cue for this particular paw, e.g. "tip" for the left paw.

6. Repeat this exercise with the other paw. When your dog understands what is required, use a verbal cue, e.g. "tap", for the right paw.

7. Avoid alternating the paws; ask for them randomly in order to stimulate your dog mentally as well as physically, and to check that he understands which paw to give.

Variations

Train the exercise with your dog in the standing position. In this way you can see exactly how your dog shifts his weight in order to compensate for the missing paw. You can intensify the effect by getting your dog to move forward. The best way to achieve this is by walking backwards while asking your dog for a paw. It is also easier if you teach your dog to touch your feet or knees instead of your hand.

Lifting and holding a paw

Lifting and holding a paw is particularly good for working the shoulder muscles and the opposing back muscles.

Use the hand target to help your dog with this excercise.

Targeted muscle groups:	Shoulder muscles, extensors and flexors of the foreleg, chest muscles, latissimus dorsi.
Suggested for:	Strengthening the shoulder muscles in particular, as well as balancing the back muscles on the other side of the dog's body.
Set-up of the exercise:	Standing next to you, your dog learns to reach out his paw to your hand and hold it up.
Prerequisite:	Giving paws, see page 67.

TRAINING STEP-BY-STEP

1. Start with your dog standing next to you and decide which paw to train.

2. Ask your dog to give this paw by offering him your hand, which he should touch. Position your hand so it is parallel to your dog's shoulder blades, and hold it high enough so that he can only touch it from underneath. Click and treat several times when your dog touches your hand from below.

3. Prolong the length of time before you click so that your dog has to hold his paw up for a longer period. Don't give up, even if it takes him a while to cotton on.

4. When your dog understands that he must maintain the position, introduce a verbal cue before you offer him your hand, e.g. "lift left".

5. Now gradually raise your hand higher so it is no longer needed as a visual aid and your dog lifts his paw on cue.

6. Repeat with the other front paw and when your dog understands what you want, introduce a cue for this side, e.g. "lift right"

Variations

1. Ask for "lift left" and "lift right" on a random basis.

2. Ask your dog take a step forward and then repeat the trick.

3. Build up the exercise so your dog is doing Spanish steps. First ask for your dog's left paw, then the right paw and vice versa. If this works, you can add forward movement by walking away from him, a step at a time.

Pushing paws against you

A good way to train this exercise is in front of the TV with your dog lying relaxed on his back. This exercise strengthens the muscles of the hind and front legs as well as the back muscles.

Initially, apply a soft counter pressure on your dog's front paws …

You can repeat this exercise, applying pressure on the hind legs.

74

Targeted muscle groups:	Shoulder muscles, sprint muscles
Suggested for:	Targeting the shoulder muscles. Balancing also uses the back muscles on the opposite side of your dog's body.
Set-up of the exercise:	While your dog is lying on his back, you offer him the palm of your hand to push against.

TRAINING STEP-BY-STEP

1. With your dog lying on his back, sit next to him. Ideally, he should be lying flat on his back, with his paws sticking up in the air.

2. Offer him a hand to push with his front paw. To get him to do this, touch his paw pads with the palm of your hand. Click and treat him for letting you touch him.

3. Now start adding a little bit of pressure. As soon as you feel your dog pushing back against you, click and treat him.

4. Repeat this several times.

5. Now gradually increase the pressure. Your dog will react in one of two ways: either he will resist the pressure and stay put, or he will push himself away gradually, sliding on his back. Either reaction is acceptable, although a dog that resists the pressure tends not to tense the shoulder muscles as much as a dog that moves.

6. Repeat this with the other front paw and with both back paws.

Down – Sit and Sit –Down

Switching between sit and down may
seem easy, but it's a great way to exercise
the forequarters and back muscles.

*Ask your dog to sit at the end of a platform – this dog needs to
be sitting more to the rear.*

Move your hand straight down to direct your dog.

Targeted muscle groups:	Shoulder muscles, extensors and flexors of the foreleg, chest muscles, latissimus dorsi.
Suggested for:	Building the muscles of the forequarters and, indirectly, the back and croup muscles. It is beneficial for young dogs as it teaches them to sit straight and to drop into the correct down position, and also for senior dogs as it gently but efficiently strengthens their muscles.
Set-up of the exercise:	Teaching your dog to switch between these positions, so that he only moves the forequarters and keeps the hindquarters in place.
What is needed:	If necessary, place your dog slightly above ground, using a platform for this purpose.

TRAINING STEP-BY-STEP

1. Ask your dog sit in front of you. If he is restless, it may help to use a platform which is big enough for him to lie down on (see page 77). Make sure you have clicker and treats to hand.

2. Working at your dog's nose level, move a treat downwards so that he has to lie down to follow it. Click and treat your dog when he is lying in a beautiful sphinx position right in front of you. Don't click if he lies with his hip sideways. If this happens, start the exercise again.

3. Now move your treat hand upwards so that he has to sit up. Hold the treat above his nose and treat him when he's sitting straight. Make sure that his hips are straight so he is sitting upright. Now click your dog in this position and treat him.

4. Repeat this position change several times, clicking and treating the end positions. Make sure that your dog goes into position quickly by increasing the speed of your hand signals.

5. Now introduce word commands for both positions. Introduce the word first and then use the hand signal. Experience has shown that it is better not to use "sit" and "down" as verbal cues if you have previously used them for the positions – but without the precision you now require. With this exercise we want to teach the correct sit and down positions.

6. Now gradually fade the hand signals and take away the platform.

Variations
Combine this change of positions with the stand and the bow. Also train this exercise on a soft surface, such as a garden lounger.

Straight Sit

Teaching your dog the straight sit is a very easy exercise which stretches the neck and back muscles.

TRAINING STEP-BY-STEP

Let your dog touch the hand target in the sit position.

Here you can control the degree of stretching by imagining a line from the tip of the nose to the tail-set. You can increase the benefit of this exercise by directing the position of the dog's nose.

Targeted muscle groups:	Shoulder muscles, latissimus dorsi.
Suggested for:	Building up the muscles of the front legs and, indirectly, working the back and croup muscles. Teaches young dogs a straight sit and is an effective method of strengthening muscles in senior dogs.
Set-up of the exercise:	Offer your sitting dog a target hand so that he has to stretch his neck fully to touch it.
Prerequisite:	Hand target

1. Ask your dog sit next to you.

2. Now offer him a target hand making sure that he stays in a sit while touching it. Hold your hand directly above his head, so that he does not feel the need to move forward. When he touches your hand, click and treat him.

3. Now move your hand in an imaginary vertical line gradually upwards. Click and treat your dog every time he touches your hand.

4. Try to move your hand upwards so that your dog doesn't just pull his head backwards but stretches his neck to the full extent. Pay attention to his forepaws. He should stretch them, and basically sit on his tiptoes.

He also needs to be sitting correctly on his hind legs, not turning them outwards and keeping them close to his body. If he turns his hind legs out, interrupt the exercise for a short time and sit him down again.

5. Prolong the sit. This exercise is strenuous and can cause muscle ache so please don't over-train.

Stand – Take A Bow

Changing from the stand into a bow is an exercise that stems from the typical 'getting up' ritual of dogs.

Targeted muscle groups:	Shoulder muscles, latissimus dorsi.
Suggested for:	Stretching the latissimus dorsi.
Set-up of the exercise:	This natural movement can become an exercise if your dog performs it on his own and you are quick to click. See below for a step-by-step guide. The exercise is not as easy as it seems, as many dogs tend to go straight into a down position.
What is needed:	Foam roller.

81

TRAINING STEP-BY-STEP

The problem with teaching this exercise is that dogs tend to go straight into the 'down' position. In order to prevent this, you will need an object, such as a foam roller, to place underneath your dog. Make sure that it is not something your dog recognises as a thing to stand on.

1. Your dog needs to stand in front of you. Next, place the roller underneath him, just in front of his back legs. Position yourself next to your dog with a clicker in one hand and a treat in the other.

2. Hold the treat high up, on a vertical line between his front legs. Drop your hand swiftly downwards. Play with different movements to find out what works best to put your dog into a bow: sometimes it helps to move the treat slightly forwards, sometimes slightly backwards. Make sure that you click the beginning of the bow, i.e. the moment when the dog lowers his front legs. Treat your dog in this position.

3. To repeat the exercise, ask your dog to stand. Use a treat if he doesn't know this command. If your dog tries to lie down on the roller under his legs, place your hand under his belly. Don't manipulate his movement, just use your hand to act as a natural barrier. Some dogs seem to enjoy this, and will lay their full body weight on to your arm. Try to stop this happening and, next time, click before he starts to lie down.

4. Gradually ask your dog to lower his body further until his elbows touch the ground. Click and treat this position several times.

5. Start fading out the treat by using your hand to lure him into position, as before, but without holding a treat. If this works, introduce a verbal cue.

6. You are now ready to remove the roller. Since your dog knows what to do, this should be no problem at all.

7. Fade out the hand signal by using the verbal command first and then giving your dog time to react without added assistance.

Variations
Although changing between positions mainly exercises the front legs, holding the position stretches the back muscles. Mix it up, depending on what you consider important. You can enhance the desired effect by teaching your dog to lie his head down on the ground or by asking him to bow down from a step or stool.

You can combine the bow with other position changes, e.g. from a down into a sit, from a sit into a stand, and from a stand into a bow.

3. Hindlimb Muscles

(plus back muscles)

Sit – Stand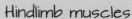

Changing from a sit to a stand is a very easy exercise that is beneficial to the hindquarters and back muscles if repeated several times.

You can use a platform to teach this exercise.

85

The alternative is to teach the stand with the dog moving backwards.

Targeted muscle groups:	Latissimus dorsi, hind extensors and flexors.
Suggested for:	Building up the muscles in the hindquarters; this is particularly beneficial for older dogs.
Set-up of the exercise:	Depending on your dog, there are two ways to train this exercise: Option 1: By offering a hand target at the right distance to cause your sitting dog to stand up. Option 2: If your dog knows how to walk backwards, you can ask him to do so when he is in a sit.
What is needed:	Platform for Option 1.
Prerequisite:	Hand target or walking backwards.

TRAINING STEP-BY-STEP

Option 1:

1. Ask your dog sit in front of you. Offer him a hand target at a sufficient distance so that he has to stand up to reach it. Make sure that he just has to stand up, and not move forward. Click and treat this behaviour.

2. **Repeat this exercise several times.**

3. Once your dog gets up expectantly before you offer your target hand, you can introduce a verbal cue.

Option 2:

1. Ask your dog stand in front of you and then cue him him to walk backwards. Click and treat him for this.

2. Repeat this several times.

3. If this works, add a verbal cue.

Tip: If your dog tends to move forward and you can't capture the stand, train this trick on an elevated surface, with your dog in the sit so that he can only stand up but not walk forward.

Tip: Timing is all-important for this exercise. When you ask him to walk backwards, click when he lifts his rear end off the ground and straightens his back legs. You want to treat him the moment he gets up and begins to move backwards.

Variations
Combine this exercise with other position changes: for example, going into a down or into a bow. This makes it more interesting and increases the benefits. Also train this exercise on soft ground.

Lifting a Hind Leg

Lifting a hind leg is especially good for teaching back-end awareness. Depending on your dog's technical level, he will be working the muscles of the thigh and the back extensors.

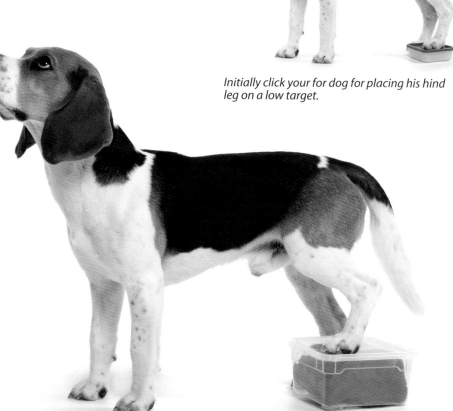

Initially click your for dog for placing his hind leg on a low target.

Exchange the low target with a higher one.

Targeted muscle groups:	Back extensors (especially longissimus dorsi), flexors and extensors of the hindquarters, croup muscles.
Suggested for:	Building hind leg muscles on one or both sides. Especially good for dogs that lack muscles in the hip area. Be careful with dogs that have knee or hip problems.
Set-up of the exercise:	In the course of training your dog will learn to use his hind leg by stepping on an elevated object such as a small box. Eventually, the target will be faded. It is important to train one leg first, and give it a verbal cue, before moving on to the next leg and giving it a different cue. It is important, however, to first train just one leg, introduce a word cue, and then start to train the other one.
What is needed:	A small box or cushion.
Prerequisite:	Walking backwards, see page 99.

TRAINING STEP-BY-STEP

For this gymnastrick, it is helpful if your dog already knows about walking backwards in a straight line, unless he is very creative in shaping exercises.

To start you need to place a small box or a cushion in front of you. Please make sure that your dog is familiar with the box or cushion and is used to walking over it.

1. Place the box/cushion so your dog is standing directly in front of it, facing you. The set-up of the exercise is similar to that of walking backwards, so your dog is likely to offer this behaviour.

2. You need to be super aware and click the moment your dog raises one hind leg. Because of the sequence of his movement, he will step on the cushion with one paw first. This will be the one you click, and this is the side you will train in the next few steps. So it is your dog who decides which leg to train first Ideally, you should capture the moment in which your dog's leg is at its highest position. If this is proving problematic, it is also fine to click when his paw touches the cushion.

TIP: In order to make this exercise easier for your dog, you can work with a barrier to the side. This helps your dog to step on to the cushion more easily, as he cannot step sideways. Just train the exercise along a wall or use broomsticks or agility poles to create a small channel.

3. If this first approach to stepping backwards on to a cushion works well, you can ask for more. There are two options:

4. You click at the moment when your dog's leg is in its highest position.

5. Or you can increase the height of the elevation, for example by putting books under the cushion. Now try to click while your dog's paw is still in the air.

There is no single training solution here; a combination of both ideas often helps to get to your goal.

6. When your dog has mastered this movement, it is time to introduce a word cue. Do this while the training aids, in form of cushions or books, are still present. Wait until you are a 100 per cent sure that your dog will show the behaviour before introducing your word cue, for example "lift" for the left hind leg.

7. Now it is time to get rid of your training aids. But if you haven't trained in different environments yet, you should do so now. Your training aids will help your dog to do this trick in different locations.

8. In order to remove the training aids, you must ask your dog to do the trick several times while they are still in place. You can then try to remove them

in an unobtrusive way. It helps to do this while your dog is eating his treats.

9. If your dog is confused, resist the temptation of helping him; it is good to give him a chance to think! However, if he appears to be getting frustrated and is making no progress, go back a step and use the training aids again until he has a solid understanding of what you want. If you intervene too quickly, you will simply be reinforcing his helplessness, which you do not want.

10. Is your dog now lifting his hind leg reliably, even when you remove the training aids? Brilliant! Now go to the spot where you last trained this exercise and try to imitate the set-up without the training aids. Depending on his character, your dog will understand what you want and offer you the behaviour directly. Otherwise, you can help him with your verbal cue. If your dog is still struggling, just go back one step.

11. Now it is time to change your position in relation to the dog. You can now stand, sit next to him or lie on the floor while asking your dog to perform the trick.

Variations

Depending on his character, your dog will show different variations of lifting his hind leg. Different muscle groups will then be targeted.

Kicking like a horse

Your dog understands the trick so well that he energetically kicks his hind leg as if he was a horse, or like a male dog after peeing. When your dog is doing the trick like this – very often he is so enthusiastic that he repeats it several times – it has the same effect as if we were to shake out our arms or legs. Therefore, it is a very good trick to relax your dog's muscles or to quickly warm them up. In order to specifically teach this variation, click the actual movement of lifting the leg, not a static position.

Peeing like a male dog

This variation is all about keeping a hind leg lifted a little bit sideways, as if your dog was peeing against a tree. If your dog is showing this variant, you can easily use this exercise for a targeted build-up of the muscles of the thigh and croup. Another option is to offer your dog your hand, so that he can push his paw against it. This increases the effect, as your hand provides counter-pressure, and it helps to boost muscular strength and endurance.

You can teach this variant by clicking him for stepping on to the elevated object and then the moment just before, so that you can capture that position.

Sit – Sitting Pretty *(beg)*

Changing from sit into a sit-pretty or beg position is an exercise that looks very easy, but it has a great effect on the mobility of the back, especially the thigh and buttocks.

TRAINING STEP-BY-STEP

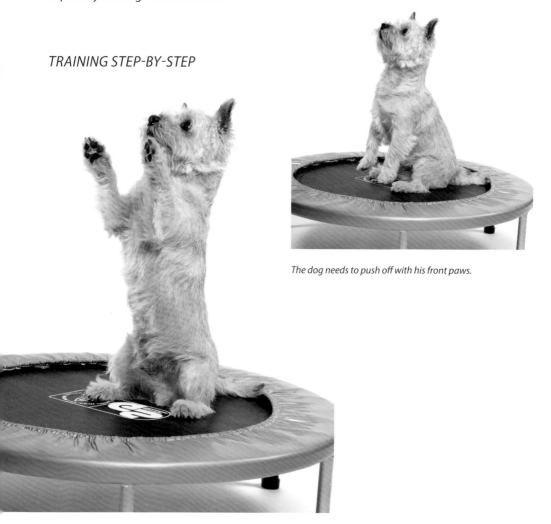

The dog needs to push off with his front paws.

'Sitting pretty' should look like this.

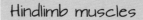

You can introduce a variation with the dog pushing off into a standing position.

The outwardly posed hind legs and hind paws show that this dog needs to improve his strength for this exercise. Problems can also occur if the floor is slippery. If your dog is struggling to balance, take extra care, progressing in small stages, to allow him to build up his muscles.

Targeted muscle groups:	Latissimus dorsi, croup muscles.
Suggested for:	Major strengthening of the back and croup muscles. Requires the dog to balance.
Set-up of the exercise:	Your dog learns to move from a sit into a sit pretty/begging position, i.e. he sits with this front paws up in the air while his bottom is on the floor.
Prerequisite:	Hand target.

93

1. Ask your dog to sit. Now briefly offer him a hand target, above the tip of his nose, so that he has to stretch up straight in order to reach it. Click and treat this movement. Repeat this several times.

2. Now start to gradually raise the hand target, so that your dog learns to push himself up with his front legs in order to reach it. Make sure he doesn't stand up, but leaves his bottom on the floor in a parallel sit, i.e. his hind legs are not turned outward to balance his weight. Only click and treat when your dog pushes up from the sit while keeping his back legs parallel.

3. If he gets up or turns his back legs outwards, interrupt the trick briefly and ask your dog to sit straight. Also, make sure your dog does not lean on your hand – you can achieve this easily by keeping a certain distance from him. This is strenuous work so take it slowly as your dog learns to balance.

4. The desired end position is when your dog can "sit pretty", without falling back into a sit or leaning on you. At this stage you can introduce a verbal command and fade out the hand signal.

Variations

You can make this exercise more effective if you train it on a soft surface, e.g. a cushion.

You can also mix up this exercise with sits. Make sure that your dog controls the movement and returns his front feet to the ground in a controlled manner. If he lets them drop, do not mix this exercise with sits until your dog has a better understanding of what he is supposed to be doing. You can intensify this exercise using the free stand (see page 97), which will strengthen the buttocks:

Sitting up-stand-up

Ask your dog to sit pretty and follow the steps of this exercise by holding the hand target directly above the tip of his nose so that he has to get into a standing position step-by-step. This is very effective for the croup muscles and hindquarters. Make sure that you give your dog enough time to balance, and gradually increase the duration of the stand.

Standing upright with help

Standing up with support is an ideal exercise for stretching the back, rear and front leg muscles. It is easy to integrate into daily life and the fact that the dog is leaning on you makes it an ideal exercise for senior dogs.

The dog is pushing off with the help of his front legs.

Targeted muscle groups:	Shoulder muscles, latissimus dorsi, rear leg flexors and extensors, croup muscles.
Suggested for:	The start of an exercise for a warm-up programme. If you massage your dog in this position, you can detect tense muscles more easily.
Set-up of the exercise:	Your dog will learn, with treats, to stand upright while leaning on you.

TRAINING STEP-BY-STEP

For this exercise you can utilise your dog's natural urge to get close to your face. Don't be afraid that this will increase his desire to jump up on people; it is easy to redirect the behaviour once you have given it a signal.

1. Encourage your dog to jump up on you. Depending on the dog, it is often enough to pat your thighs or to get his interest by using a treat and moving it up along your body. If your dog tends to jump up on you generally, capture this behaviour with a verbal signal and click and treat him for this.

2. Reinforce this exercise by training it in different places.

Variations
Ask your dog to jump up on you on different surfaces or from an elevated platform or a step so you can change the distance, and therefore the angle, of his position.

Standing Upright Without Help

Standing upright without support trains your dog's sense of balance and his back-end awareness. This is an easy exercise to train but it does take time for your dog to perfect his balance so he can stand without assistance.

For this exercise the front paws, rather than the head, are directed towards the target. Therefore the muscles of the front paws are stretched instead of the nuchal ligament.

Targeted muscle groups:	Nuchal band, latissimus dorsi, hind leg flexors and extensors.
Suggested for:	Building the muscles of the hind legs.
Set-up of the exercise:	Offer your dog a target he has to reach up to so that he learns to balance himself.

TRAINING STEP-BY-STEP

1. Ask your dog to stand in front of you. Offer him a hand target or a high value treat.

2. Raise it so that your dog has to stand upright to follow it. Click the first upright stand and treat your dog in this position

3. Click your dog five times in this position.

4. Take a break! This exercise is very tiring for your dog.

5. You can now start to hold your treat hand so high that your dog has to reach up with his head in order to get it. Click and treat when he reaches up, and let your dog "suck" the treat in this position for a little while. While he is licking the treat, watch his back legs.

6. If your dog has to walk around to balance himself, keep practising until he stands up in a controlled manner. Once he demonstrates that he can do this without hesitation, you can introduce a verbal cue.

7. Now you can start moving your hand further away from your dog, so that he has no direct target to aim for. Play around with height and distance, changing the angle at which he has to stretch his neck.

Variations

Train this exercise with your dog standing on a soft surface, which will enhance the effect on the thigh muscles. I would discourage you from asking your dog to move forward in this position, as all of his weight will be put on to one leg, and many dogs will start to jump, which is not beneficial for their skeletal structure.

Walking backwards in a straight line

To teach this exercise, you need to sit in a chair and place a mat in front of you.

Place a treat under the chair and encourage your dog to find it, making sure he goes between your legs.

... your dog will come out backwards from beneath the chair.

Click your dog for touching the mat with both hind paws.

Increase the distance by moving the chair. The target remains in its initial position. Your dog is now walking backwards in a straight line, which demands a great deal of co-ordination.

In order to make your dog aware of his hind legs, try using bandages.

Targeted muscle groups:	Latissimus dorsi, hind leg flexors and extensors, sprint muscles.
Suggested for:	Working on your dog's body awareness and his co-ordination, particularly of the hind legs.
Set-up of the exercise:	By using a target mat that your dog learns to touch with his hind legs, you can teach him to walk backwards in a perfectly straight line.
What is needed:	A mat that is not much wider than your dog; a chair.

TRAINING STEP-BY-STEP

1. Place a mat in front of a chair, leaving a gap the length of your dog between the two of you. When he is standing directly in front of you, his hind legs should be on the mat.

2. Sit on the chair, and ask your dog to stand in front of you. If necessary, adjust the mat.

3. Place a treat under the chair so that your dog has to take both back legs off the mat in order to get the treat. Now it gets interesting…

Note: If your dog tries to walk forward, you have placed the treat too far away from him. You can prevent forwards movement by blocking him off to the front and to the side, with a cushion, for example.

4. With clicker and treats at the ready, capture the moment when your dog walks backwards and has to step on to the mat. Treat your dog while his back legs are on the mat.

5. Repeat the above steps at least 10 times.

6. Now change the distance between the chair and the mat – but remember that the target mat always stays in the same place.

7. Proceed in small steps so that your dog has to move just a little bit more each time. Click and treat when your dog is standing on the mat. Treat him there and only there, even if you have to get up from the chair to do so.

8. Once you can move at least a body length away from your dog and he is

moving in a straight line on the mat, you can gradually increase the distance between the chair and target mat. You are now ready to phase out the chair. Do this gradually, sitting closer and closer to the edge of the chair, and eventually standing up. Gradually increase the distance between the chair and target mat, and then you are ready to phase out the chair. Do this gradually, sitting closer and closer to the edge, and eventually standing up.

9. Once your dog understands this exercise, repeat it two or three times and then take away the target mat for a couple of goes before replacing it. This teaches your dog to walk backwards without a target.

NOTE: If your dog tends to walk backwards at an angle, it may be that he has a favourite side, just like we have a favourite leg to jump on. It could also be that his muscles are stronger or weaker on one side. You may need to check to see if he has tense muscles or any other muscular issues.

To encourage your dog to walk backwards in a straight line, you can put poles on either side of the walkway. Make sure you click only when he is standing with both hind legs on the mat. Make sure you don't treat from the same hand; use both hands to prevent one-sided expectation.

Down – take a bow

This exercise is a great workout for the hind leg muscles and also stretches the back muscles.

Get yourself and your dog into this position.

With the help of your hand, your dog will learn to lift his rear end.

Targeted muscle groups:	Latissimus dorsi, hind leg flexors and extensors.
Suggested for:	Stretching your dog's back muscles while training his hindquarters. Ideal for young and senior dogs.
Set-up of the exercise:	Using the down position as a starting point, you teach your dog to lift his rear end.

TRAINING STEP-BY-STEP

1. Sit on the floor with your legs forming a V in front of you; ask your dog to lie down between your legs.

2. Now move your open hand in front of your dog's chest and wait for a reaction. If he moves his back legs here, click and treat this movement. If not, carefully move your open hand underneath your dog's chest in order to get him to move. Click even the tiniest of movements.

3. Play around with the position of your hand and wait longer before you click so that your dog has to increase his movement to earn a treat. Once your dog has moved into the desired position, give an extra special treat to mark the behaviour you are looking for.

4. Repeat this several times and then give a verbal cue.

5. Now you can start to fade out the hand signal.

Variations
You can combine this exercise with the down, for example, to enhance the stretch effect.

4. All Muscles

Crawling

Crawling strengthens the front, rear and back muscles; it is only recommended for healthy dogs without injuries or health issues.

Click for the first interest in the post-it.

… and shape a movement by slowly going backwards.

Targeted muscle groups:	Shoulder muscles, front leg extensors and flexors, chest muscles, latissimus dorsi, hind leg extensors and flexors, croup muscles.
Suggested for:	An all-round warm-up, but as it works all the muscles and is quite strenuous, your dog will need to do some initial warm-up exercises.
Set-up of the exercise:	Starting from the down position, use post-its as paw targets to encourage your dog to crawl.
What is needed:	Post-its.

TRAINING STEP-BY-STEP

1. Ask your dog to go into the down position. Now, with the clicker at the ready, attach a post-it to your foot and stand in front of your dog.

2. Click as soon as he shows any interest in your foot. Ideally he will touch your foot with his paw, but it is acceptable if he uses his nose.

3. Click and treat your dog for showing interest several times.

4. Now you can start slowly moving backwards, first only half a step. Your dog will try to follow you. Click and treat this movement. Make sure that you only treat your dog when he is in the down position in order to prevent him getting up.

5. Proceed step-by-step until he can do several steps without being treated in between. Your dog will develop his very own crawling technique!

6. Add a verbal command.

7. Fade out the post-it by reducing its size.

8. Vary your position in relation to your dog.

Variations

You can achieve a better muscle workout if your dog crawls underneath objects. Don't overdo it – and only teach your dog to crawl if he is sound and healthy.

Balancing a bowl on the back

Like balancing a bowl on the head (see page 61), your dog needs to have very good body awareness and perception to perform this exercise.

In order to begin this exercise, teach your dog to stand despite touching him.

Now you can use a flat-based item, such as a bowl, to balance on your dog's back.

Slowly fade out your 'hold' hand.

Now lure your dog forwards.

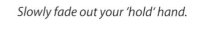

Targeted muscle groups:	Latissimus dorsi, hind leg extensors and flexors, croup muscles.
Suggested for:	Training the dog's awareness and use of his back end.
Set-up of the exercise:	You will need to teach the 'hold' trick first (see page 51) and then get your dog accustomed to balancing an item on his rear end.
What is needed:	A lightweight, flat-based item such as a bowl or a tray that is small enough to stay in position on your dog's back.
Prerequisite:	The 'hold' trick.

TRAINING STEP-BY-STEP

1. Sit on a chair with your dog standing in front of you. Offer your hand and ask for "hold", i.e. placing his head in the palm of your hand (see page 51); click and treat him for this.

2. "Hold" is only a tool that teaches your dog to stand still even when you touch him, so you need to train this. Ask him to "hold" while gently touching his bottom. Click and treat him while he is standing still.

3. If this works, you can place the bowl. First, touch your dog's rear end with the bowl, but don't let go. Click and treat your dog for remaining still. If your dog doesn't like the bowl being placed on his back, apply gentle pressure with your hand only so that he learns to stand still.

4. Once your dog is OK with the bowl touching his back, you can gradually start to let go of it. Click and treat your dog for this.

5. Introduce a verbal cue when you place the bowl on his back.

6. You can fade out the "hold" command when your dog understands that he must remain still when the bowl is placed on his back. Be generous with your treats for this intermediate step.

7. You are now ready to add the most difficult element – movement. Offer your dog a target hand as an incentive to simply shift his weight at first. If he does this without letting the bowl fall from his back, treat him handsomely. If he lets the bowl fall, keep on trying.

8. Proceed, literally step-by-step, to encourage your dog to move while he balances the bowl on his back. You are now ready to join the circus!

Going upstairs backwards

Going up the stairs backwards requires a great deal of coordination from your dog. It is also very tiring and only recommended for perfectly healthy dogs. Lifting the back legs strengthens their muscles, but the front legs are subjected to stress, since much of the dog's weight is being shifted on to them.

Start with your dog in a stand.

Now encourage your dog to walk backwards.

You can use a barrier to keep your dog in line with the steps.

Here you can see the sequence of movement required for ascending the steps backwards.

113

Targeted muscle groups:	Shoulder muscles, front leg extensors and flexors, chest muscles, latissimus dorsi, hind leg extensors and flexors.
Suggested for:	A quick warm-up for all parts of the body but should only be used for perfectly healthy dogs and not as the starting point of a warm-up programme.
Set-up of the exercise:	Starting from walking backwards, you will teach your dog to step up on to something which will lead to stair climbing.
What is needed:	Stairs, firm cushions or variously sized shoe boxes.
Prerequisite:	Walking backwards, see page 99.

TRAINING STEP-BY-STEP

1. Start by asking your dog to walk backwards on his own several times and treat this.

2. Now add something at a slight elevation behind your dog which he can step on to. For this you can use a dog step, a flat shoebox or a box lid. Make sure that the elevated object cannot slip.

3. Ask your dog to walk backwards again. He might initially be confused about the object, which is why you should click and treat the moment he touches it.

4. Repeat this several times but do not click until your dog has put at least one paw on to the object.

5. Keep working until he has put both paws on the object.

6. Now you are ready to introduce another step, so that you have a two step element. Using your walking backwards command, encourage your dog to move from the first level of elevation on to the second.

7. If this works, you can introduce a new verbal cue that tells the dog to climb upstairs backwards.

8. Repeat this exercise in different places. Integrate 'natural' objects, such as real steps or logs.

Walking Consciously

Walking consciously may not seem like much of a trick, but it is very important as it teaches your dog to focus on taking every step deliberately.

Walking at a single pace for a longer period of time will reveal inconsistencies in the dog's gait.

Here you can see how the dog has to balance lifting his right foreleg by moving his left hind leg. Very often the least impressive-looking exercises have the greatest effect.

Targeted muscle groups:	Shoulder muscles, front leg extensors and flexors, chest muscles, latissimus dorsi, hind leg extensors and flexors, sprint muscles.
Suggested for:	All dogs: young or old, healthy or not. It has a relaxing effect and is useful for pinpointing tension in the muscles.
Set-up of the exercise:	By walking slowly with your dog, you will train his awareness of where and how to place his paws.

TRAINING STEP-BY-STEP

Train this exercise when your dog is not too excited and make sure you have clicker and treats at the ready. You also need to decide which foot you are going to focus on first.

1. Ask your dog to stand next to you, and take a step forwards. Be very vigilant and click as soon as your dog moves one paw. Treat your dog in this exact position.

2. Now you and your dog have to move the other foot forward as well. Experiment to find the perfect step length so that your dog can place his paw next to yours. Treat your dog in this position.

3. Repeat on both sides, literally step-by-step, in order to establish this behaviour. Then introduce a verbal command.

Tip: If your dog has trouble understanding this movement, teach him to see your foot as a target that he has to touch. Start by asking him to touch your foot with a paw, using post-its.

Variations
Vary the length of your stride so that your dog has to adjust his paces, which increases the workout.

Change of pace: walk-trot, trot-walk

Changing pace from walking to trotting is a workout for you as you have to guide your dog during this process.

Here you can see how the dog decreases his speed coming out of the trot.

When your dog is starting to trot, click and reward him for the change of pace so he understands what is required.

Targeted muscle groups:	Shoulder muscles, front leg extensors and flexors, chest muscles, latissimus dorsi, hind leg extensors and flexors, sprint muscles.
Suggested for:	A short training exercise while out on a walk, it is ideal for raising awareness of both body and gait. It can also be used to detect muscle tension.
Set-up of the exercise:	Have your dog on a lead and encourage him to move at the same pace as you. Click when you change gait and establish a verbal command.
What is needed:	Lead.

TRAINING STEP-BY-STEP

1. Put your dog on a lead and encourage him to adjust his pace to yours. Walk very slowly, so that your dog has to keep pace.

2. If this works, increase your speed slightly and get ready to click. Click as soon as your dog changes from walking to trotting.

3. Walk a few metres at trotting pace and then slow down again. Click when your dog changes from trotting to walking. Walk a few metres at this pace.

4. Repeat the transitions several times, making sure your dog changes and adjusts his pace accordingly. Do not control your dog by using the lead. If he is struggling to adjust to your pace, help him with a treat.

5. Once the change between gaits is smooth, you can introduce a verbal cue, for example "walk" and "trot".

6. Generalise this exercise. Train it without a lead, on a bicycle or with your dog on a lunge line.

Variations
To achieve the best effect, train this exercise on different terrains, such as a springy sports field, in the forest or on hard asphalt.

Looking Straight Ahead While Moving Forward

Many exercises require your dog to be focused on you, but this exercise is intended to train the exact opposite behaviour: to teach your dog to move forward independently.

To begin with, only send your dog on a short distance.

Gradually increase the distance.

Now you have shaped a movement where your dog consciously looks ahead.

Targeted muscle groups:	Shoulder muscles, front leg extensors and flexors, chest muscles, latissimus dorsi, hind leg extensors and flexors, sprint muscles.
Suggested for:	Offsetting walking at heel and preventing one-sided muscular stress. Enhances a natural, loose and springy forwards movement.
Set-up of the exercise:	Using a target/feeding station at the same height as your dog's head, you can teach him fairly quickly to move forward while keeping his head turned straight ahead.
What is needed:	Target/feeding station at the same height as your dog's head.

TRAINING STEP-BY-STEP

If your dog is quite motivated, use a post-it to trigger this trick and then treat. If your dog needs to be motivated, use food straight away.

1. Place the post-it or the food on a stool or an object that is at the same height as your dog's head. Move your dog approximately 1.5 body lengths away from the target.

2. With clicker and treats ready, show the dog his target. Make sure that you only click when your dog looks at the target with his head straight ahead.

3. Increase the distance to the target and click every time your dog holds his head straight forward, and at different distances to the target.

4. Introduce a verbal cue.

5. Now make the target more and more inconspicuous, e.g. by hiding it between pieces of furniture. Remove the target for a couple of repetitions and see what happens. Make it as easy as possible for your dog and behave as you would if the target was there.

6. Generalise this exercise by training it in different places.

Variations
You can increase the benefits if you train your dog on springy ground.

Stepping Underneath

This exercise is difficult to teach as it requires great observational skills. A horse riding background could help you here.

This dog is showing a wonderful trot. The best time to click is the phase of the trot in which the paws of one side are at the greatest distance from each other.

To recognise a powerful canter is more complicated so focus on the out-stretched legs. Click at this phase, or when your dog is preparing to push, depending on which can be more easily detected.

Targeted muscle groups:	Shoulder muscles, front leg extensors and flexors, chest muscles, latissimus dorsi, hind leg extensors and flexors, sprint muscles.
Suggested for:	Enhancing power in movement by teaching the dog to stretch his legs as far as he can (trot) and bending his back (canter). Ideal for rehabilitation after a rest period.
Set-up of the exercise:	Your dog walks next to you in the chosen gait und you teach collected movement.
What is needed:	If necessary, a bicycle.

TRAINING STEP-BY-STEP

You need to get an idea of what 'collected' movement should look like. Collection means that your dog deliberately steps under his centre of gravity without tensing up, moving forward gracefully and changing between flexed muscles and free movement. Think of the movement of a dressage horse that neither pulls up its head nor drops it. This is not controlled by the rider; the horse puts all its power, strength and vibrancy into the movement.

Once you can see this picture take your dog, on a lead, into an open field, with clicker and treats at the ready. Ideally, you should be walking or running alongside your dog, or you could use a bicycle.

1. Move at your desired pace. Pay attention to your dog and vary your pace.

2. Click when your dog shows the first signs of collection. It is easier if your dog is trotting or cantering instead of walking. He will lengthen out his trot, stepping well within his centre of gravity when he is just about to change into the canter. So when you sense that your dog is lengthening his trot, this is the right moment. Click and treat your dog while he is moving and repeat the exercise.

3. In the canter movement, the right moment is usually the phase between the change from trotting to a full canter. Look for a regular and rhythmic forward and downward motion and a loose neck. Click and treat during the movement.

4. It is usually easier to produce the lengthened out trot when working in a straight line, whereas your dog is more likely to show the collected canter when running a big circle.

5. In this exercise, it will be difficult to get away from the body signal of walking next to your dog. However, do introduce a verbal cue as this will make it easier to change between gaits.

5. Intensifying The Tricks

Holding An Object

In order to intensify the gymnastricks, you can teach your dog to hold an object in his mouth, irrespective of whatever else he is doing. Use your dog's favourite toy to start off with. Then you can try something heavier: the 'retrieve' articles used in obedience or field trials are ideal, because you can get them in different sizes and shapes. You can even find objects where you can adjust the weight with the help of small, lead balls. Do not ask for too much and make sure you ask your vet or physiotherapist if this is a good option for your dog.

By adding an extra element, such as holding a retrieve article, the dog gets more of a workout.

Holding and carrying an object is a trick that is complex. Do not give up if it does not work out straightaway: keep trying! Teaching this exercise can take a month and there are dogs who will never really enjoy retrieving, which is something you should accept.

There are numerous ways of teaching your dog how to hold and carry an article and the following guide is just one suggestion.

TRAINING STEP-BY-STEP

1. Sit in front of or next to your dog, holding the retrieve article. Make the article interesting by showing it to your dog and playing with it.

2. Now move the article around, level with your dog's head, and click for the tiniest interest in it.

3. You can then shape this interest by only clicking and rewarding when your dog is using his muzzle.

4. If this works, withhold the click long enough so that your dog starts to open his mouth. Click this immediately and reward with lots of praise and treats.

5. From here on in, you need to shape the action of taking the article in his mouth. Be very generous with your rewards.

6. Once your dog holds the article in his mouth, withhold the click in order to add duration.

7. If this works, you can then add a verbal cue for holding the article.

8. In order to solidify his learning, tap the side of the article and reward your dog for holding it.

9. Offer your dog a treat directly in front of his nose, above the article – a treat that he can only earn by holding the article for a longer time.

10. You can now add movement. Walk with your dog and offer him the article while walking. If he takes it, that earns him a click and a reward. Add duration here as well.

11. You can now start to give the article to your dog just before asking for a gymnastrick.

Bandages

Another way to increase the effectiveness of the gymnastricks programme is to use bandages. They are also very helpful if your dog's muscles are more developed on one side than the other. You can buy bandages fitted with different weights, but this is not always necessary. You need to be aware that weight bandages influence not only the leg concerned but also the whole body. This is one of the reasons why you should check with your vet or physiotherapist to see if the use of weight bandages is advised for your dog: otherwise, you could harm him rather than help him.

The weight of the bandages can be varied.

Different Surfaces

Different surfaces not only stimulate your dog, they can also help to increase the training effect. Especially useful are soft surfaces that 'give' under the weight of your dog, such as trampolines, mattresses, deck chairs with fabric seating or a sofa.

You can also train outside, using different terrain, and surfaces. In addition, you can increase the effect by training the exercises on a gymnastic cushion, which works the muscles and improves balance.

More effort is required for sitting up on a balance cushion.

A combination of 'down' and 'stand' is hard work when it is performed on two cushions.

A trampoline increases the effectives of a trick, such as this 'sit-stand'.

Acknowledgements

This book and all my knowledge, not only about specific exercises but especially about independent, not to say, stubborn dogs can be credited to my now 13-year old Beagle, Lou. For the last five years, Darwin, our little clown, has enriched our pack. Without my two lads, I would have never been able to learn so much about dogs. Lou's illness and his never ending joy of life motivated me to dig through specialised literature in order to make his life as joyous as possible. And Darwin's reproachful looks, when I was sitting too long in front of my laptop, have always reminded me to take a break. Both of them complement each other in the best possible way and I am so lucky to have them.